Summing Up a Pet's Needs

by Ali Butler
illustrated by Susan Swan

 HOUGHTON MIFFLIN   BOSTON

Printed in China

ISBN 10: 0-618-89986-3
ISBN 13: 978-0-618-89986-9

456789 0940 16 15 14 13
4500411355

It's not fair! My parents promised me that I could have a puppy if I saved enough money. So I saved up $35 because that's what the animal shelter charges for adopting a pet. But now my parents tell me that I also have to buy the other things that a puppy will need.

$17?

$24?

$8?

They say a puppy needs a dog crate, a collar, a leash, food and water bowls, a grooming brush, and puppy shampoo. That could cost $70! How will I ever get all that money?

Mom and Dad know I'm upset because I stormed out of the kitchen when I heard the news. They called for me to come back, but I pretended I had turned off my hearing aids and couldn't hear them.

This was supposed to be my best summer ever. Now it's turning out to be the worst.

Read·Think·Write If a puppy costs $35 to adopt and Rosa needs about $70 for the extra items, how much will she need altogether?

3

Today was a little better than yesterday. My abuela and I had a really good talk this morning after my parents left for work.

Abuela said, "It is your summer vacation. You'll have lots of time to earn the extra money you need."

I told her I didn't even know how much money I needed. How much does a dog crate cost? What about a leash? Food and water bowls? In my mind, it was a hopeless situation. I might as well give up my dream of owning a dog.

But my grandmother refused to let me give up. She told me that when people really want something, sometimes they have to work very hard to make sure they get it. She also told me that she had a plan.

Abuela explained that the first thing we had to do was figure out how much money I needed to buy the pet supplies. She told me that I could do that by finding the approximate cost of each item. I didn't have to know the exact cost—I just needed to be close.

Next, she handed me a few weekly ads from the local pet store. She told me to look through them and find out about how much each item costs. Then she said that when we know about how much each item costs, we can add them together to find out about how much the total will be.

I can't wait to get started!

Read·Think·Write If three items on Rosa's list cost about $2, $5, and $4, what would be her total cost for all three items?

When I walked into the kitchen this morning, I was greeted by the wonderful aroma of cinnamon. My abuela had made churros for breakfast. She always knows how to make me feel better.

As we ate our breakfast, we looked over the list I had completed last night.

Abuela said that now I had an estimate, or good guess, of the cost of each item. To get the total cost of all the items, Abuela suggested that we round the numbers first, so they would be easier to add.

She pointed out that every item cost some dollars and some cents. She said that if the cents were less than 50, then we would round down to the nearest dollar. If the cents were more than 50, then we would round up to the nearest dollar. It sounded kind of complicated, but after Abuela helped me write it out, it made sense.

	Actual Cost	Rounded Number
Crate	$24.75	$25.00
Collar	$ 3.39	$ 3.00
Leash	$ 3.75	$ 4.00
Water and food bowls	$ 4.09	$ 4.00
Brush	$ 2.79	$ 3.00
Shampoo	$ 2.49	$ 2.00

Then we added the rounded numbers and arrived at our total estimate.

I'll have to work hard to earn all that money!

Read·Think·Write Add the rounded numbers. What is Rosa's total estimate?

I've been working so hard to earn the $41 that I haven't had time to write in my journal!

These past two weeks, I raked Mrs. Irving's yard. I walked the huge dog that belongs to the Chavez family. While Mr. and Mrs. Thomas were on vacation, I fed their cats. I also washed dishes for Mr. Vega while he recovered from knee surgery. And because everyone was so thankful, they paid me really well. I made more than $50!

This morning Mom and Dad told me that they were proud of all the work I had done to earn the money I needed. They liked the way I went to the neighbors, asked them if they needed help with any chores, and then worked for them.

But then Dad began to talk about the cost of dog food and visits to the veterinarian, and I started to panic.

They must have seen the scared look on my face because my father suddenly said, "Don't worry, Rosa!" He said that he and Mom would pay for the puppy's food and medical bills.

I was happy once again—tomorrow we could pick up my puppy!

Oh, I almost forgot. Abuela taught me something really cool about addition. She said that no matter what order I add the numbers from the list, I will still get the same total. I looked this up in my math book—and she was right! It's a rule called the commutative property of addition. This rule says: The sum of two or more numbers will always be the

$$\$25.00 + \$3.00 + \$4.00 + \$4.00 + \$3.00 + \$2.00 = \$41$$
$$\$4.00 + \$3.00 + \$25.00 + \$3.00 + \$2.00 + \$4.00 = \$41$$

same, no matter in what order you add them.

Grandmothers sure are smart!

Read·Think·Write How much is $5 + 6 + 2$? How much is $6 + 2 + 5$?

July 8

Today is the day!

We went to the animal shelter this morning and I had a surprise. The black and white puppy that I had seen three weeks ago was gone! Someone had adopted the puppy only yesterday!

I couldn't believe it. My puppy was gone! I sat on the floor and started to cry.

Suddenly, a wiggly yellow furball pounced onto my lap. The puppy started licking away my tears. A shelter volunteer said, "He just arrived yesterday and he's full of energy. Here, let me get him off you."

But the puppy didn't want to leave me.

"I think this puppy likes you," my grandmother said.

And you know what? She was right again! I now estimate that this puppy and I are going to be best friends for a very long time.

1. **Recognize a Main Idea** Which of the following, when rounded, would equal $25.00?

   A. $24.15
   B. $24.49
   C. $24.55

2. Which of the following shows the commutative property of addition?

   A. $2 + 3 = 5$ and $3 + 2 = 5$
   B. $6 + 1 = 7$ and $5 + 2 = 7$
   C. $1 + 4 = 5$ and $4 + 5 = 9$

3. How would you estimate the total cost of a list of items for a pet?

Activity

Look at a print ad from a grocery store. Make a list of your favorite foods and their prices. Then round each price to the nearest ten cents and make a second list. Which list is easier for you to add in your head?